THE EARLY YEARS FOUNDATION STAGE

Sara Miller McCune founded SAGE Publishing in 1965 to support the dissemination of usable knowledge and educate a global community. SAGE publishes more than 1000 journals and over 800 new books each year, spanning a wide range of subject areas. Our growing selection of library products includes archives, data, case studies and video. SAGE remains majority owned by our founder and after her lifetime will become owned by a charitable trust that secures the company's continued independence.

Los Angeles | London | New Delhi | Singapore | Washington DC | Melbourne

THE EARLY YEARS FOUNDATION STAGE

Learning Matters
A SAGE Publishing Company
1 Oliver's Yard
55 City Road
London EC1Y 1SP

SAGE Publications Inc.
2455 Teller Road
Thousand Oaks, California 91320

SAGE Publications India Pvt Ltd
B 1/l 1 Mohan Cooperative Industrial Area
Mathura Road
New Delhi 110 044

SAGE Publications Asia-Pacific Pte Ltd
3 Church Street
#10-04 Samsung Hub
Singapore 049483

Editor: Amy Thornton
Senior project editor: Chris Marke
Cover design: Wendy Scott
Typeset by: C&M Digitals (P) Ltd, Chennai, India
Printed in the UK

Library of Congress Control Number: 2021942042

British Library Cataloguing in Publication Data

A catalogue record for this book is available from
the British Library

ISBN 978-1-5297-4147-6 (pbk)

At SAGE we take sustainability seriously. Most of our products are printed in the UK using responsibly sourced papers
and boards. When we print overseas we ensure sustainable papers are used as measured by the PREPS grading
system. We undertake an annual audit to monitor our sustainability.

CONTENTS

ABOUT THIS BOOK

This book presents the Statutory Framework for the Early Years Foundation Stage. This guidance was published on 31 March 2021 by the Department for Education.

It can be found online here:

https://assets.publishing.service.gov.uk/government/uploads/ system/uploads/attachment_data/file/974907/EYFS_framework_-_ March_2021.pdf

Other documents published by the Department for Education in relation to the Early Years Foundation Stage can be found here:

https://www.gov.uk/education/early-years-curriculum

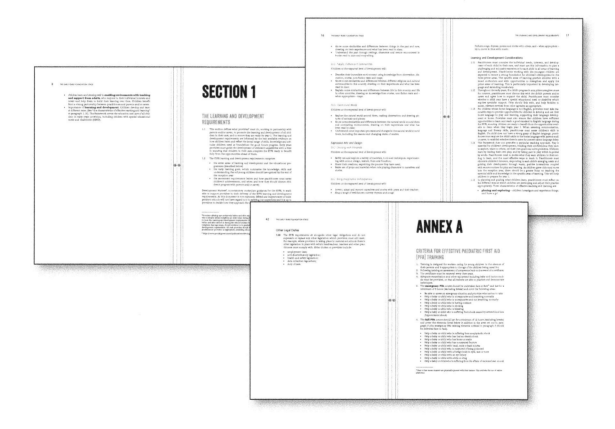

In the Foreword, Aaron Bradbury explores how this statutory framework relates to practice in early years settings. He outlines what the EYFS is, what it is not and how effective practitioners use this as a framework upon which to build their practice and focus their understanding of children's learning.

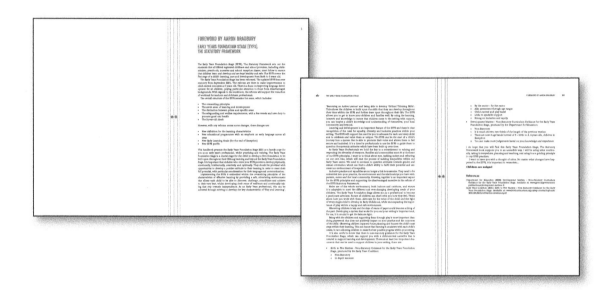

At the end of the book, a full and detailed index of the document is included. This is a useful tool for practice as it allows students and practitioners a detailed reference guide for this key document.

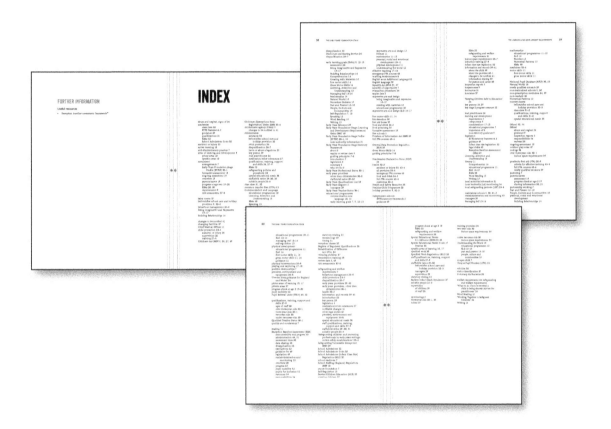

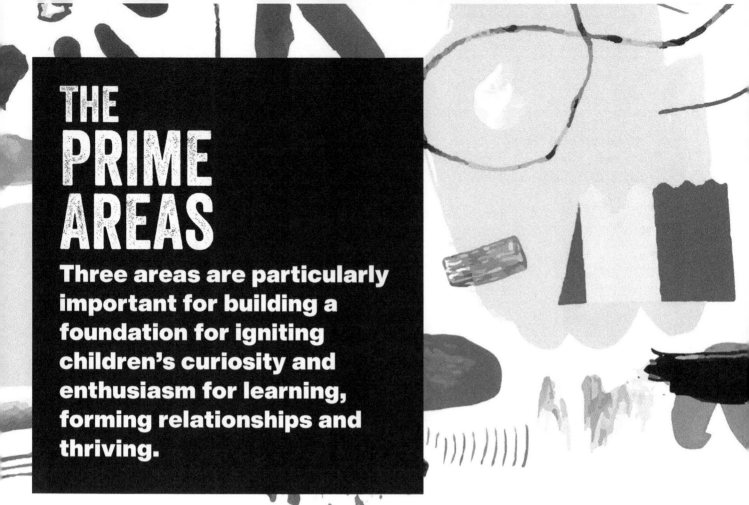

Three areas are particularly important for building a foundation for igniting children's curiosity and enthusiasm for learning, forming relationships and thriving.

Communication and Language

The development of children's spoken language underpins all seven areas of learning and development.

Physical Development

Physical activity is vital in children's all-round development, enabling them to pursue happy, healthy and active lives.

Personal, social and emotional development

Children's personal, social and emotional development (PSED) is crucial for children to lead healthy and happy lives, and is fundamental to their cognitive development.

THE SPECIFIC AREAS

Providers must also support children in four specific areas, through which the three prime areas are strengthened and applied.

Key Words for Expressive arts and design

- artistic and cultural awareness
- imagination and creativity
- engage with the arts
- explore and play
- media and materials
- quality and variety
- see, hear and participate
- self-expression
- communicate through the arts
- interpreting and appreciating
- respond to
- observe

Key Words for Mathematics

- a strong grounding in number
- building blocks
- excel mathematically
- count confidently
- deep understanding
- patterns within
- numbers
- build and apply
- using manipulatives
- organising counting
- vocabulary
- rich opportunities
- spatial reasoning skills
- positive attitudes
- interest in mathematics
- look for patterns
- spot connections
- not afraid to make mistakes

Key Words for Literacy

- a life-long love of reading
- language comprehension
- word reading
- starts from birth
- adults talk with children
- stories and non-fiction books
- rhymes, poems and songs
- enjoy reading together
- pronunciation familiar printed words
- transcription composition
- before writing
- articulating ideas the
- world around them

Key Words for Understanding the world

- make sense
- physical world
- community
- personal experiences
- knowledge
- sense
- world around them
- visiting parks
- important members of society
- broad selection of stories
- understanding
- culturally, socially, technologically and ecologically diverse world
- familiarity with words
- enriching
- widening

FOREWORD BY AARON BRADBURY

EARLY YEARS FOUNDATION STAGE (EYFS), THE STATUTORY FRAMEWORK

The Early Years Foundation Stage (EYFS), The Statutory Framework sets out the standards that all Ofsted registered childcare and school providers, including child-minders, preschools, nurseries and school reception classes, must follow to ensure that children learn and develop and are kept healthy and safe. The EYFS covers the first stage of a child's learning, care and development from birth to 5 years old.

The Early Years Foundation Stage has been reformed. The updated EYFS becomes statutory from September 2021. The reforms are there to make improvements to child centred outcomes at 5 years old. There is a focus on improving language development for all children, paying particular attention to those from disadvantaged backgrounds. With regards to the workforce, the reforms will support the reduction of workload for teachers and childcare professionals.

The overall structure of the EYFS remains the same, which includes:

- The overarching principles
- The seven areas of learning and development
- The distinction between prime and specific areas
- The safeguarding and welfare requirements, with a few tweaks and new duty to promote good oral health
- The 2-year-old check

However, with any reforms comes some changes, these changes are:

- New definition for the learning characteristics
- New educational programmes with an emphasis on early language across all areas
- New Early Learning Goals (for the end of Reception)
- New EYFS profile

This handbook presents the Early Years Foundation Stage 2021 as a handy copy for you as an early year's professional, whilst practicing and training. The Early Years Foundation Stage is a crucial stage for the child to develop a firm foundation to be built upon throughout their lifelong learning and beyond the Early Years Foundation Stage. It is important that children who enter your EYFS provision develop physically, emotionally, intellectually, creatively and spiritually. They should be provided with opportunities to develop a positive attitude to their learning in order to meet their full potential, with particular consideration for their language and communication.

Implementing the EYFS is embedded within the overarching principles of the characteristics of effective learning by providing a safe, stimulating environment that allows each child to be able to discover, challenge, consolidate and achieve to their very best, whilst developing their sense of resilience and continually taking that step towards independence. As an Early Years professional, this can be achieved through striving to develop the key characteristics of 'Play and Learning',

'Becoming an Active Learner' and being able to develop 'Critical Thinking Skills'. This allows the children to build upon the skills that they can develop throughout their time within the EYFS and further draw upon throughout their life. The EYFS allows you to get to know your children and families well. By using the learning, interests and knowledge to ensure that children come to the setting with support, you can inspire a child's knowledge and understanding of themselves, your local community and beyond.

Learning and development is an important feature of the EYFS and there is clear recognition of the need for equality, diversity and inclusive practices within your setting. The EYFS will support the need for you to advocate for each and every child and to celebrate and value them as unique. The EYFS can be the start of a child's journey into a system that is able to promote their voice and allows them to feel secure and included. It is a time for professionals to use the EYFS to guide them to question the systemic attitudes which have been built up over time.

As Early Years Professionals we hold the key to a commitment to valuing and respecting the diversity of everyone. Families and communities must sit at the heart of our EYFS principles. I want us to think about race, tackling racism and reflecting on our own bias, which will start the process of tackling inequalities within our Early Years sector. We need to continue to question attitudes towards gender and sexual orientation which can limit a child's ability to fulfil their potential and can create an environment of inequality.

Inclusive practice and equalities are no longer a tick box exercise. They need to be embedded into your practice, the environment and the relationships you have with parents, carers and the local community. Growing together is an important aspect for the EYFS principles and supporting the disadvantaged narrative in the reform of the EYFS Statutory Framework.

Make use of the whole environment, both indoors and outdoors, and ensure it is adaptable to meet the different and ever-changing developing needs of your children. The Early Years Foundation Stage allows you as a professional to become a passionate advocate. Ensure all children can share with you how they feel. Think about how you work with them. Advocate for the voice of the child and the right of every single child to develop in Early Childhood, while encompassing the importance of play within a happy and safe environment.

Observing children is key and the days of reams of paper could become a thing of the past. Developing a system that works for you and your setting is important and, for me, it is crucial to get the balance right.

Being with the children and supporting them through play is more important than doing paperwork that does not positively impact on your practice and the outcomes of the child. Observing children supports future planning and focuses the child's next steps within their learning. This can ensure that learning is consistent with each child's needs, in turn allowing children to make the best possible progress within your setting.

It is also useful to know that there is non-statutory guidance for the Early Years Foundation Stage, which can support you with a child-centred narrative that is needed to support learning and development. There are at least two important documents that can be used to support children in your setting, these are:

- Birth to Five Matters - Non-Statutory Guidance for the Early Years Foundation Stage, produced by the Early Years Coalition:
  - Non-Statutory
  - In depth resource

o   By the sector – for the sector
o   Aids assessment through age ranges
o   Child-centred and play based
o   Links to specialist support
o   Strong on inclusion and equity

- Development Matters – Non-Statutory Curriculum Guidance for the Early Years Foundation Stage, produced by the Department for Education:

o   Non-Statutory
o   It is much shorter, two thirds of the length of the previous version
o   There are now 3 age bands instead of 6 – birth to 3, 4-year-olds, children in Reception
o   You can make more judgements based on your knowledge and experience

I do hope that you will find this Early Years Foundation Stage, The Statutory Framework book supports you in an accessible way. I will be using mine continually, taking it everywhere, planning and teaching, and using it as a guiding principle to my EYFS practices.

I want to leave you with a thought of mine. No matter what changes have happened in the EYFS, it is important to remember…

Children are unique!

References

Department for Education (2020) Development Matters – Non-Statutory Curriculum Guidance for the Early Years Foundation Stage. Available at: www.gov.uk/government/publications/development-matters--2

Early Years Coalition (2021) Birth to Five Matters – Non-Statutory Guidance for the Early Years Foundation Stage. Available at: www.birthto5matters.org.uk/wp-content/uploads/2021/03/Birthto5Matters-download.pdf

STATUTORY FRAMEWORK FOR THE EARLY YEARS FOUNDATION STAGE

SETTING THE STANDARDS FOR LEARNING, DEVELOPMENT AND CARE FOR CHILDREN FROM BIRTH TO FIVE

Published: 31 March 2021

Effective: 1 September 2021

CONTENTS

SUMMARY

About this statutory framework

This framework is mandatory for all early years providers in England from 1 September 2021[1].

Ofsted and inspectorates of independent schools have regard to the Early Years Foundation Stage (EYFS) in carrying out inspections and report on the quality and standards of provision. Ofsted publishes inspection reports at www.gov.uk/ofsted. Ofsted may issue actions (in respect of any failure to meet a requirement in the document) and/or may issue a welfare requirements notice (in respect of Section 3). It is an offence for a provider to fail to comply with a welfare requirements notice. Early years childminder agencies are also under a duty to have regard to the EYFS in the exercise of their functions.

The learning and development requirements in sections 1 and 2 of this framework, and the safeguarding and welfare requirements in section 3 of this framework, are indicated by the use of the word "must". Additionally, early years providers must "have regard" to other provisions in these sections. These provisions are indicated by the use of the word "should". "Having regard" to these provisions means that early years providers must take them into account when providing early years provision and should not depart from them unless there is good reason for doing so.

Expiry or review date

This framework remains in force until further notice.

What legislation does this framework refer to?

- The learning and development requirements are given legal force by an Order[2] made under section 39(1)(a) of the Childcare Act 2006
- The safeguarding and welfare requirements are given legal force by Regulations[3] made under section 39(1)(b) of the Childcare Act 2006

Who is this framework for?

This framework is for all early years providers in England (from 1 September 2021): maintained schools; non-maintained schools; independent schools (including free schools and academies); all providers on the Early Years Register; and all providers registered with an early years childminder agency (CMA).[4]

---

[1]Section 46 of the Childcare Act 2006 enables the Secretary of State to confer exemptions from the learning and development requirements in certain prescribed circumstances.

[2]The Early Years Foundation Stage (Learning and Development Requirements) Order 2007 (S.I. 2007/1772), as amended.

[3]The Early Years Foundation Stage (Welfare Requirements) Regulations 2012 (S.I. 2012/938), as amended.

[4]The Childcare (Exemptions from Registration) Order 2008 (S.I.2008/979) specifies the circumstances in which providers are not required to register.

INTRODUCTION

1. Every child deserves the best possible start in life and the support that enables them to fulfil their potential. Children develop quickly in the early years and a child's experiences between birth and age five have a major impact on their future life chances. A secure, safe and happy childhood is important in its own right. Good parenting and high quality early learning together provide the foundation children need to make the most of their abilities and talents as they grow up.

2. The Early Years Foundation Stage (EYFS) sets the standards that all early years providers must meet to ensure that children learn and develop well and are kept healthy and safe. It promotes teaching and learning to ensure children's 'school readiness' and gives children the broad range of knowledge and skills that provide the right foundation for good future progress through school and life.

3. The EYFS seeks to provide:

   - **quality and consistency** in all early years settings, so that every child makes good progress and no child gets left behind
   - **a secure foundation** through planning for the learning and development of each individual child, and assessing and reviewing what they have learned regularly
   - **partnership working** between practitioners and with parents and/or carers
   - **equality of opportunity** and anti-discriminatory practice, ensuring that every child is included and supported

4. The EYFS specifies requirements for learning and development and for safeguarding children and promoting their welfare. The **learning and development requirements** cover:

   - the **areas of learning and development** which must shape activities and experiences (**educational programmes**) for children in all early years settings
   - the **early learning goals** that providers must help children work towards (the knowledge, skills and understanding children should have at the end of the academic year in which they turn five)
   - **assessment arrangements** for measuring progress (and requirements for reporting to parents and/or carers)

5. The **safeguarding and welfare requirements** cover the steps that providers must take to keep children safe and promote their welfare.

Overarching principles

6. Four guiding principles should shape practice in early years settings. These are:

   - every child is a **unique child**, who is constantly learning and can be resilient, capable, confident and self-assured
   - children learn to be strong and independent through **positive relationships**

- children learn and develop well in **enabling environments with teaching and support from adults,** who respond to their individual interests and needs and help them to build their learning over time. Children benefit from a strong partnership between practitioners and parents and/or carers.
- importance of **learning and development.** Children develop and learn at different rates. (See "the characteristics of effective teaching and learning" at paragraph 1.15). The framework covers the education and care of all children in early years provision, including children with special educational needs and disabilities (SEND).

SECTION 1

THE LEARNING AND DEVELOPMENT REQUIREMENTS

1.1   This section defines what providers[5] must do, working in partnership with parents and/or carers, to promote the learning and development of all children in their care, and to ensure they are ready for year 1. The learning and development requirements are informed by the best available evidence on how children learn and reflect the broad range of skills, knowledge and attitudes children need as foundations for good future progress. Early years providers must guide the development of children's capabilities with a view to ensuring that children in their care complete the EYFS ready to benefit fully from the opportunities ahead of them.

1.2   The EYFS learning and development requirements comprise:

- the seven areas of learning and development and the educational programmes (described below)
- the early learning goals, which summarise the knowledge, skills and understanding that all young children should have gained by the end of the reception year
- the assessment requirements (when and how practitioners must assess children's achievements, and when and how they should discuss children's progress with parents and/or carers)

Development Matters[6], non-statutory curriculum guidance for the EYFS, is available to support providers in their delivery of the EYFS learning and development requirements. As this document is non-statutory, Ofsted and inspectorates of independent schools will not have regard to it in carrying out inspections and it is up to providers to decide how they approach the curriculum.

---

[5]Providers offering care exclusively before and after school or during the school holidays for children who normally attend reception (or older) class during the school day (see paragraph 3.41) do not need to meet the learning and development requirements. However, providers offering care exclusively before and after school or during the school holidays for children younger than those in the reception class age range, should continue to be guided by, but do not have to meet, the learning and development requirements. All such providers should discuss with parents and/or carers (and other practitioners/providers as appropriate, including school staff/teachers) the support they intend to offer.

[6] https://www.gov.uk/government/publications/development-matters--2

The areas of learning and development

1.3   There are seven areas of learning and development that must shape educational programmes in early years settings. All areas of learning and development are important and inter-connected.

1.4   Three areas are particularly important for building a foundation for igniting children's curiosity and enthusiasm for learning, forming relationships and thriving.

These are the **prime areas**:

- communication and language
- physical development
- personal, social and emotional development

1.5   Providers must also support children in four specific areas, through which the three prime areas are strengthened and applied. The **specific** areas are:

- literacy
- mathematics
- understanding the world
- expressive arts and design

Educational Programmes

1.6   Educational programmes must involve activities and experiences for children, as set out under each of the areas of learning.

Communication and Language

The development of children's spoken language underpins all seven areas of learning and development. Children's back-and-forth interactions from an early age form the foundations for language and cognitive development. The number and quality of the conversations they have with adults and peers throughout the day in a language-rich environment is crucial. By commenting on what children are interested in or doing, and echoing back what they say with new vocabulary added, practitioners will build children's language effectively. Reading frequently to children, and engaging them actively in stories, non-fiction, rhymes and poems, and then providing them with extensive opportunities to use and embed new words in a range of contexts, will give children the opportunity to thrive. Through conversation, storytelling and role play, where children share their ideas with support and modelling from their teacher, and sensitive questioning that invites them to elaborate, children become comfortable using a rich range of vocabulary and language structures.

Personal, Social and Emotional Development

Children's personal, social and emotional development (PSED) is crucial for children to lead healthy and happy lives, and is fundamental to their cognitive development. Underpinning their personal development are the important attachments that shape their social world. Strong, warm and supportive relationships with adults enable children to learn how to understand their own feelings and those of others. Children should be supported to manage emotions, develop a positive sense of self, set themselves simple goals, have confidence in their own abilities, to persist and wait for what they want and direct attention as necessary. Through adult modelling and guidance, they will learn how to look after their bodies, including healthy eating, and manage personal needs independently. Through supported interaction with other children, they learn how to make good friendships, co-operate and resolve conflicts peaceably. These attributes will provide a secure platform from which children can achieve at school and in later life.

Physical Development

Physical activity is vital in children's all-round development, enabling them to pursue happy, healthy and active lives[7]. Gross and fine motor experiences develop incrementally throughout early childhood, starting with sensory explorations and the development of a child's strength, co-ordination and positional awareness through tummy time, crawling and play movement with both objects and adults. By creating games and providing opportunities for play both indoors and outdoors, adults can support children to develop their core strength, stability, balance, spatial awareness, co-ordination and agility. Gross motor skills provide the foundation for developing healthy bodies and social and emotional well-being. Fine motor control and precision helps with hand-eye co-ordination, which is later linked to early literacy. Repeated and varied opportunities to explore and play with small world activities, puzzles, arts and crafts and the practice of using small tools, with feedback and support from adults, allow children to develop proficiency, control and confidence.

Literacy

It is crucial for children to develop a life-long love of reading. Reading consists of two dimensions: language comprehension and word reading. Language comprehension (necessary for both reading and writing) starts from birth. It only develops when adults talk with children about the world around them and the books (stories and non-fiction) they read with them, and enjoy rhymes, poems and songs together. Skilled word reading, taught later, involves both the speedy working out of the pronunciation of unfamiliar printed words (decoding) and the speedy recognition of familiar printed words. Writing involves transcription (spelling and handwriting) and composition (articulating ideas and structuring them in speech, before writing).

Mathematics

Developing a strong grounding in number is essential so that all children develop the necessary building blocks to excel mathematically. Children should be able to count confidently, develop a deep understanding of the numbers to 10, the relationships between them and the patterns within those numbers. By providing frequent

---

[7]The Chief Medical Officer has published guidance on physical activity, which is available at: https://www.gov.uk/government/publications/physical-activity-guidelines-uk-chief-medical-officers-report.

and varied opportunities to build and apply this understanding – such as using manipulatives, including small pebbles and tens frames for organising counting – children will develop a secure base of knowledge and vocabulary from which mastery of mathematics is built. In addition, it is important that the curriculum includes rich opportunities for children to develop their spatial reasoning skills across all areas of mathematics including shape, space and measures. It is important that children develop positive attitudes and interests in mathematics, look for patterns and relationships, spot connections, 'have a go', talk to adults and peers about what they notice and not be afraid to make mistakes.

Understanding the World

Understanding the world involves guiding children to make sense of their physical world and their community. The frequency and range of children's personal experiences increases their knowledge and sense of the world around them – from visiting parks, libraries and museums to meeting important members of society such as police officers, nurses and firefighters. In addition, listening to a broad selection of stories, non-fiction, rhymes and poems will foster their understanding of our culturally, socially, technologically and ecologically diverse world. As well as building important knowledge, this extends their familiarity with words that support understanding across domains. Enriching and widening children's vocabulary will support later reading comprehension.

Expressive Arts and Design

The development of children's artistic and cultural awareness supports their imagination and creativity. It is important that children have regular opportunities to engage with the arts, enabling them to explore and play with a wide range of media and materials. The quality and variety of what children see, hear and participate in is crucial for developing their understanding, self-expression, vocabulary and ability to communicate through the arts. The frequency, repetition and depth of their experiences are fundamental to their progress in interpreting and appreciating what they hear, respond to and observe.

Early Learning Goals

1.7   The level of development children should be expected to have attained by the end of the EYFS is defined by the early learning goals (ELGs) as set out below.

1.8   The ELGs should not be used as a curriculum or in any way to limit the wide variety of rich experiences that are crucial to child development, from being read to frequently to playing with friends.

1.9   Instead, the ELGs should support teachers[8] to make a holistic, best-fit judgement about a child's development, and their readiness for year 1.

1.10   When forming a judgement about whether an individual child is at the expected level of development, teachers should draw on their knowledge of

---

[8]Teacher should be understood to refer to any practitioner working with the child.

the child and their own expert professional judgement. This is sufficient evidence to assess a child's individual level of development in relation to each of the ELGs. Sources of written or photographic evidence are not required, and teachers are not required to record evidence.

Communication and Language

ELG: Listening, Attention and Understanding

Children at the expected level of development will:

- Listen attentively and respond to what they hear with relevant questions, comments and actions when being read to and during whole class discussions and small group interactions;
- Make comments about what they have heard and ask questions to clarify their understanding;
- Hold conversation when engaged in back-and-forth exchanges with their teacher and peers.

ELG: Speaking

Children at the expected level of development will:

- Participate in small group, class and one-to-one discussions, offering their own ideas, using recently introduced vocabulary;
- Offer explanations for why things might happen, making use of recently introduced vocabulary from stories, non-fiction, rhymes and poems when appropriate;
- Express their ideas and feelings about their experiences using full sentences, including use of past, present and future tenses and making use of conjunctions, with modelling and support from their teacher.

Personal, Social and Emotional Development

ELG: Self-Regulation

Children at the expected level of development will:

- Show an understanding of their own feelings and those of others, and begin to regulate their behaviour accordingly;
- Set and work towards simple goals, being able to wait for what they want and control their immediate impulses when appropriate;
- Give focused attention to what the teacher says, responding appropriately even when engaged in activity, and show an ability to follow instructions involving several ideas or actions.

ELG: Managing Self

Children at the expected level of development will:

- Be confident to try new activities and show independence, resilience and perseverance in the face of challenge;
- Explain the reasons for rules, know right from wrong and try to behave accordingly;
- Manage their own basic hygiene and personal needs, including dressing, going to the toilet and understanding the importance of healthy food choices.

ELG: Building Relationships

Children at the expected level of development will:

- Work and play cooperatively and take turns with others;
- Form positive attachments to adults and friendships with peers;
- Show sensitivity to their own and to others' needs.

Physical Development

ELG: Gross Motor Skills

Children at the expected level of development will:

- Negotiate space and obstacles safely, with consideration for themselves and others;
- Demonstrate strength, balance and coordination when playing;
- Move energetically, such as running, jumping, dancing, hopping, skipping and climbing.

ELG: Fine Motor Skills

Children at the expected level of development will:

- Hold a pencil effectively in preparation for fluent writing – using the tripod grip in almost all cases;
- Use a range of small tools, including scissors, paint brushes and cutlery;
- Begin to show accuracy and care when drawing.

Literacy

ELG: Comprehension

Children at the expected level of development will:

- Demonstrate understanding of what has been read to them by retelling stories and narratives using their own words and recently introduced vocabulary;
- Anticipate – where appropriate – key events in stories;
- Use and understand recently introduced vocabulary during discussions about stories, non-fiction, rhymes and poems and during role-play.

ELG: Word Reading

Children at the expected level of development will:

- Say a sound for each letter in the alphabet and at least 10 digraphs;
- Read words consistent with their phonic knowledge by sound-blending;
- Read aloud simple sentences and books that are consistent with their phonic knowledge, including some common exception words.

ELG: Writing

Children at the expected level of development will:

- Write recognisable letters, most of which are correctly formed;
- Spell words by identifying sounds in them and representing the sounds with a letter or letters;
- Write simple phrases and sentences that can be read by others.

Mathematics

ELG: Number

Children at the expected level of development will:

- Have a deep understanding of number to 10, including the composition of each number;
- Subitise (recognise quantities without counting) up to 5;
- Automatically recall (without reference to rhymes, counting or other aids) number bonds up to 5 (including subtraction facts) and some number bonds to 10, including double facts.

ELG: Numerical Patterns

Children at the expected level of development will:

- Verbally count beyond 20, recognising the pattern of the counting system;
- Compare quantities up to 10 in different contexts, recognising when one quantity is greater than, less than or the same as the other quantity;
- Explore and represent patterns within numbers up to 10, including evens and odds, double facts and how quantities can be distributed equally.

Understanding the World

ELG: Past and Present

Children at the expected level of development will:

- Talk about the lives of the people around them and their roles in society;

- Know some similarities and differences between things in the past and now, drawing on their experiences and what has been read in class;
- Understand the past through settings, characters and events encountered in books read in class and storytelling.

ELG: People, Culture and Communities

Children at the expected level of development will:

- Describe their immediate environment using knowledge from observation, discussion, stories, non-fiction texts and maps;
- Know some similarities and differences between different religious and cultural communities in this country, drawing on their experiences and what has been read in class;
- Explain some similarities and differences between life in this country and life in other countries, drawing on knowledge from stories, non-fiction texts and – when appropriate – maps.

ELG: The Natural World

Children at the expected level of development will:

- Explore the natural world around them, making observations and drawing pictures of animals and plants;
- Know some similarities and differences between the natural world around them and contrasting environments, drawing on their experiences and what has been read in class;
- Understand some important processes and changes in the natural world around them, including the seasons and changing states of matter.

Expressive Arts and Design

ELG: Creating with Materials

Children at the expected level of development will:

- Safely use and explore a variety of materials, tools and techniques, experimenting with colour, design, texture, form and function;
- Share their creations, explaining the process they have used;
- Make use of props and materials when role playing characters in narratives and stories.

ELG: Being Imaginative and Expressive

Children at the expected level of development will:

- Invent, adapt and recount narratives and stories with peers and their teacher;
- Sing a range of well-known nursery rhymes and songs;

Perform songs, rhymes, poems and stories with others, and – when appropriate – try to move in time with music.

Learning and Development Considerations

1.11   Practitioners must consider the individual needs, interests, and development of each child in their care, and must use this information to plan a challenging and enjoyable experience for each child in all areas of learning and development. Practitioners working with the youngest children are expected to ensure a strong foundation for children's development in the three prime areas. The specific areas of learning provide children with a broad curriculum and with opportunities to strengthen and apply the prime areas of learning. This is particularly important in developing language and extending vocabulary.

1.12   Throughout the early years, if a child's progress in any prime area gives cause for concern, practitioners must discuss this with the child's parents and/or carers and agree how to support the child. Practitioners must consider whether a child may have a special educational need or disability which requires specialist support. They should link with, and help families to access, relevant services from other agencies as appropriate.

1.13   For children whose home language is not English, providers must take reasonable steps to provide opportunities for children to develop and use their home language in play and learning, supporting their language development at home. Providers must also ensure that children have sufficient opportunities to learn and reach a good standard in English language during the EYFS, ensuring children are ready to benefit from the opportunities available to them when they begin year 1. When assessing communication, language and literacy skills, practitioners must assess children's skills in English. If a child does not have a strong grasp of English language, practitioners must explore the child's skills in the home language with parents and/or carers, to establish whether there is cause for concern about language delay.

1.14   This framework does not prescribe a particular teaching approach. Play is essential for children's development, building their confidence as they learn to explore, relate to others, set their own goals and solve problems. Children learn by leading their own play, and by taking part in play which is guided by adults. Practitioners need to decide what they want children in their setting to learn, and the most effective ways to teach it. Practitioners must stimulate children's interests, responding to each child's emerging needs and guiding their development through warm, positive interactions coupled with secure routines for play and learning. As children grow older and move into the reception year, there should be a greater focus on teaching the essential skills and knowledge in the specific areas of learning. This will help children to prepare for year 1.

1.15   In planning and guiding what children learn, practitioners must reflect on the different rates at which children are developing and adjust their practice appropriately. Three characteristics of effective teaching and learning are:

- **playing and exploring** – children investigate and experience things, and 'have a go'

- **active learning** – children concentrate and keep on trying if they encounter difficulties, and enjoy achievements
- **creating and thinking critically** – children have and develop their own ideas, make links between ideas, and develop strategies for doing things

1.16 Each child must be assigned a key person[9] (also a safeguarding and welfare requirement – see paragraph 3.27). Providers must inform parents and/or carers of the name of the key person, and explain their role, when a child starts attending a setting. The key person must help ensure that every child's learning and care is tailored to meet their individual needs. The key person must seek to engage and support parents and/or carers in guiding their child's development at home. They should also help families engage with more specialist support if appropriate.

1.17 A quality learning experience for children requires a quality workforce. A well-qualified, skilled staff strongly increases the potential of any individual setting to deliver the best possible outcomes for children. Requirements in relation to staff qualifications are outlined in Section 3.

---

[9]In childminding settings, the key person is the childminder.

SECTION 2

ASSESSMENT

2.1 Assessment plays an important part in helping parents, carers and practitioners to recognise children's progress, understand their needs, and to plan activities and support. Ongoing assessment (also known as formative assessment) is an integral part of the learning and development process. It involves practitioners knowing children's level of achievement and interests, and then shaping teaching and learning experiences for each child reflecting that knowledge. In their interactions with children, practitioners should respond to their own day-to-day observations about children's progress and observations that parents and carers share.

2.2 Assessment should not entail prolonged breaks from interaction with children, nor require excessive paperwork. When assessing whether an individual child is at the expected level of development, practitioners should draw on their knowledge of the child and their own expert professional judgement and should not be required to prove this through collection of physical evidence.

2.3 Parents and/or carers should be kept up-to-date with their child's progress and development. Practitioners should address any learning and development needs in partnership with parents and/or carers, and any relevant professionals. Assessment should inform an ongoing dialogue between practitioners and year 1 teachers about each child's learning and development, to support a successful transition to key stage 1.

Progress check at age two

2.4 When a child is aged between two and three, practitioners must review their progress, and provide parents and/or carers with a short written summary of their child's development in the prime areas. This progress check must identify the child's strengths, and any areas where the child's progress is less than expected. If there are significant emerging concerns, or an identified special educational need or disability, practitioners should develop a targeted plan to support the child's future learning and development involving parents and/or carers and other professionals (for example, the provider's Special Educational Needs Co-ordinator (SENCO) or health professionals) as appropriate.

2.5 Beyond the prime areas, it is for practitioners to decide what the written summary should include, reflecting the development level and needs of the individual child. The summary must highlight: areas in which a child is progressing well; areas in which some additional support might be needed; and focus particularly on any areas where there is a concern that a child may have a developmental delay (which may indicate a special educational need or disability). It must describe the activities and strategies the provider intends to adopt to address any issues or concerns. If a child moves settings between the ages of two and three it is expected that the progress check would usually be undertaken by the setting where the child has spent most time. Practitioners must discuss with parents and/or carers how the summary of development can be used to support learning at home.

2.6   Practitioners should encourage parents and/or carers to share information from the progress check with other relevant professionals, including their health visitor and the staff of any new provision the child may transfer to. Practitioners must agree with parents and/or carers when will be the most useful point to provide a summary. Where possible, the progress check and the Healthy Child Programme health and development review at age two (when health visitors gather information on a child's health and development) should inform each other and support integrated working. This will allow health and education professionals to identify strengths as well as any developmental delay and any particular support from which they think the child/family might benefit. Providers must have the consent of parents and/or carers to share information directly with other relevant professionals.

Assessment at the start of the reception year – the Reception Baseline Assessment (RBA)

2.7   The Reception Baseline Assessment (RBA) is a short assessment, taken in the first six weeks in which a child starts reception.

2.8   The statutory guidance for the administration of the RBA is set out in Annex B. The guidance covers all intakes in reception within an academic year including during autumn, spring and summer terms.

Assessment at the end of the EYFS – the Early Years Foundation Stage Profile (EYFSP)

2.9   In the final term of the year in which the child reaches age five, and no later than 30 June in that term, the EYFS Profile must be completed for each child. This includes those children who, by exception, complete the EYFS in an Ofsted or childminder agency registered setting and who are due to start school in year 1 in the following academic year.

2.10   The Profile provides parents and carers, practitioners and teachers with a well-rounded picture of a child's knowledge, understanding and abilities, their attainment against expected levels, and their readiness for year 1. The Profile must reflect practitioners' own knowledge and professional judgement of a child to inform discussions with parents and carers, and any other adults whom the teacher, parent or carer judges can offer a useful contribution.

2.11   Each child's level of development must be assessed against the early learning goals (see Section 1). Practitioners must indicate whether children are meeting expected levels of development, or if they are not yet reaching expected levels ('emerging'). This is the EYFS Profile.

2.12   Year 1 teachers must be given a copy of the Profile report. Reception teachers, or early years practitioners where the Profile has been completed for a child who has remained in Ofsted registered early years provision, may choose to provide a short commentary on each child's skills and abilities in relation to the three key characteristics of effective teaching and learning (see paragraph 1.15). These should help inform a dialogue between reception and year 1 teachers about each child's stage of development and learning needs and assist with the planning of activities in year 1.

2.13   Schools[10] must share the results of the Profile with parents and/or carers, and explain to them when and how they can discuss the Profile with the teacher[11] who completed it. For children attending more than one setting, the Profile must be completed by the school where the child spends most time. If a child moves to a new school during the academic year, the original school must send their assessment of the child's level of development against the early learning goals to the relevant school within 15 days of receiving a request. If a child moves during the summer term, relevant providers must agree which of them will complete the Profile.

2.14   The Profile must be completed for all children, including those with special educational needs or disabilities (SEND). Reasonable adjustments to the assessment process for children with SEND must be made as appropriate. Providers should consider whether they may need to seek specialist assistance to help with this. Children will have differing levels of knowledge, skills and abilities across the Profile and it is important that there is a full assessment of all areas of their development, to inform plans for future activities and to identify any additional support needs.

Information to be provided to the local authority

2.15   Early years providers must report EYFS Profile results to local authorities, upon request.[12] Local authorities are under a duty to return this data to the relevant Government department.

---

[10]Or the relevant provider.

[11]Or other practitioner.

[12]Childcare (Provision of Information about Young Children (England) Regulations 2009.

SECTION 3

THE SAFEGUARDING AND WELFARE REQUIREMENTS

Introduction

3.1   Children learn best when they are healthy, safe and secure, when their individual needs are met, and when they have positive relationships with the adults caring for them. The safeguarding and welfare requirements, specified in this section, are designed to help providers create high quality settings which are welcoming, safe and stimulating, and where children are able to enjoy learning and grow in confidence.

3.2   Providers must take all necessary steps to keep children safe and well. The requirements in this section explain what early years providers must do to: safeguard children; ensure the suitability of adults who have contact with children; promote good health; manage behaviour; and maintain records, policies and procedures.

3.3   Schools are not required to have separate policies to cover EYFS requirements provided the requirements are already met through an existing policy. Where providers other than childminders are required to have policies and procedures as specified below, these policies and procedures should be recorded in writing. Childminders are not required to have written policies and procedures. However, they must be able to explain their policies and procedures to parents, carers, and others (for example Ofsted inspectors or the childminder agency with which they are registered) and ensure any assistants follow them.

Child protection

3.4   Providers must be alert to any issues of concern in the child's life at home or elsewhere. Providers must have and implement a policy, and procedures, to safeguard children. These should be in line with the guidance and procedures of the relevant local safeguarding partners (LSP). The safeguarding policy and procedures must include an explanation of the action to be taken when there are safeguarding concerns about a child and in the event of an allegation being made against a member of staff, and cover the use of mobile phones and cameras in the setting. To safeguard children and practitioners online, providers will find it helpful to refer to 'Safeguarding children and protecting professionals in early years settings: online safety considerations'[13]

3.5   A practitioner must be designated to take lead responsibility for safeguarding children in every setting. Childminders must take the lead responsibility themselves. The lead practitioner is responsible for liaison with local statutory children's services agencies, and with the LSP. They must provide support, advice and guidance to any other staff on an ongoing basis, and on any specific safeguarding issue as required. The lead practitioner must attend a child protection training course[14] that enables them to identify, understand and respond appropriately to signs of possible abuse and neglect (as described at paragraph 3.6).

3.6   Providers must train all staff to understand their safeguarding policy and procedures, and ensure that all staff have up to date knowledge of safeguarding issues. Training made available by the provider must enable staff to identify signs of possible abuse and neglect at the earliest opportunity, and to respond in a timely and appropriate way. These may include:

- significant changes in children's behaviour
- deterioration in children's general well-being
- unexplained bruising, marks or signs of possible abuse or neglect
- children's comments which give cause for concern
- any reasons to suspect neglect or abuse outside the setting, for example in the child's home or that a girl may have been subjected to (or is at risk of) female genital mutilation[15] and/or
- inappropriate behaviour displayed by other members of staff, or any other person working with the children, for example: inappropriate sexual comments; excessive one-to-one attention beyond the requirements of their usual role and responsibilities; or inappropriate sharing of images

Providers may also find 'What to do if you're worried a child is being abused: Advice for practitioners'[16] helpful.

3.7   Providers must have regard to the government's statutory guidance 'Working Together to Safeguard Children'[17] and to the 'Prevent duty guidance for England and Wales'[18]. All schools are required to have regard[19] to the government's 'Keeping Children Safe in Education'[20] statutory guidance, and other childcare providers may also find it helpful to refer to this guidance. If providers have concerns about children's safety or welfare, they must notify agencies

---

[13]https://www.gov.uk/government/publications/safeguarding-children-and-protecting-professionals-in-early-years-settings-online-safety-considerations

[14]Taking account of any advice from the LSP or local authority on appropriate training courses.

[15]https://www.gov.uk/government/collections/female-genital-mutilation

[16]https://www.gov.uk/government/publications/what-to-do-if-youre-worried-a-child-is-being-abused--2

[17]https://www.gov.uk/government/publications/working-together-to-safeguard-children--2

[18]The 2015 Counter Terrorism and Security Act places a duty on early years providers "to have due regard to the need to prevent people from being drawn into terrorism" (the Prevent duty): www.gov.uk/government/publications/prevent-duty-guidance/revised-prevent-duty-guidance-for-england-and-wales

[19]Under section 175(4) of the Education Act 2002

[20]www.gov.uk/government/publications/keeping-children-safe-in-education--2

with statutory responsibilities without delay. This means the local children's social care services and, in emergencies, the police.

3.8. Registered providers must inform Ofsted or their childminder agency of any allegations of serious harm or abuse by any person living, working, or looking after children at the premises (whether the allegations relate to harm or abuse committed on the premises or elsewhere). Registered providers must also notify Ofsted or their childminder agency of the action taken in respect of the allegations. These notifications must be made as soon as is reasonably practicable, but at the latest within 14 days of the allegations being made. A registered provider who, without reasonable excuse, fails to comply with this requirement, commits an offence.

Suitable people

3.9   Providers must ensure that people looking after children are suitable to fulfil the requirements of their roles. Providers must have effective systems in place to ensure that practitioners, and any other person who may have regular contact with children (including those living or working on the premises), are suitable[21].

3.10 Ofsted or the agency with which the childminder is registered is responsible for checking the suitability of childminders, of every other person looking after children for whom the childminding is being provided, and of every other person living or working on any domestic premises from which the childminding is being provided, including requiring enhanced criminal records checks and barred list checks. Registered providers other than childminders and childcare on domestic premises must obtain an enhanced criminal records check in respect of every person aged 16 and over (including for unsupervised volunteers, and supervised volunteers who provide personal care[22]) who[23]:

- works directly with children
- lives on the premises on which the childcare is provided (unless there is no access to the part of the premises when and where children are cared for) and/or
- works on the premises on which the childcare is provided (unless they do not work on the part of the premises where the childcare takes place, or do not work there at times when children are present)

An additional criminal records check (or checks if more than one country) should also be made for anyone who has lived or worked abroad[24].

---

[21]To allow Ofsted or the relevant childminder agency to make these checks, childminders are required to supply information to Ofsted or the relevant childminder agency, as set out in Schedule 1, Part 2 of the Childcare (Early Years Register) Regulations 2008, amended by the Childcare (Early Years Register) (Amendment) Regulations 2012. The requirements relating to people who live and work on childminder premises are in Schedule 1, Part 1.

[22]Personal care includes helping a child, for reasons of age, illness or disability, with eating or drinking, or in connection with toileting, washing, bathing and dressing.

[23]The requirement for a criminal records check will be deemed to have been met in respect of all people living or working in childcare settings, whose suitability was checked by Ofsted or their local authority before October 2005.

[24]See: www.gov.uk/government/publications/criminal-records-checks-for-overseas-applicants

3.11   Providers must tell staff that they are expected to disclose any convictions, cautions, court orders, reprimands and warnings[25] that may affect their suitability to work with children (whether received before or during their employment at the setting). Providers must not allow people, whose suitability has not been checked, including through a criminal records check[26], to have unsupervised contact with children being cared for.

3.12   Providers other than childminders must record information about staff qualifications and the identity checks and vetting processes that have been completed (including the criminal records check reference number, the date a check was obtained and details of who obtained it). For childminders, the relevant information will be kept by Ofsted or the agency with which the childminder is registered.

3.13   Providers must also meet their responsibilities under the Safeguarding Vulnerable Groups Act 2006, which includes a duty to make a referral to the Disclosure and Barring Service where a member of staff is dismissed (or would have been, had the person not left the setting first) because they have harmed a child or put a child at risk of harm[27].

Disqualification

3.14   A provider or a childcare worker may be disqualified from registration[28]. In the event of the disqualification of a provider, the provider must not continue as an early years provider – nor be directly concerned in the management of such provision. Where a person is disqualified, the provider must not employ that person in connection with early years provision. Where an employer becomes aware of relevant information that may lead to disqualification of an employee, the provider must take appropriate action to ensure the safety of children.

3.15   A childminder, childminder assistant or a childcare practitioner working on domestic premises may also be disqualified because they live in the same household as another person who is disqualified, or because they live in the same household where a disqualified person is employed. If a childminder, childminder assistant or childcare practitioner is disqualified they may, in some circumstances, be able to obtain a 'waiver' from Ofsted.

3.16   A registered provider must notify Ofsted or the agency with which the childminder is registered of any significant event which is likely to affect the

---

[25]Except convictions or cautions that are protected for the purposes of the Rehabilitation of Offenders Act 1974.

[26]DBS disclosures and barred list information are only issued to the potential employee; providers must check the disclosure and consider whether it contains any information that would suggest the person was unsuitable for the position, before an individual has unsupervised contact with children. Where a potential or existing employee has subscribed to the online DBS Update service, providers should check the status of the disclosure. Where the check identifies there has been a change to the disclosure details, a new enhanced DBS disclosure must be applied for. Before accessing the DBS update service consent to do so must be obtained from the member of staff.

[27]Section 35 of the Safeguarding Vulnerable Groups Act 2006.

[28]In accordance with regulations made under Section 75 of the Childcare Act 2006. Schools are required to have regard to the disqualification guidance published by the Department for Education, which is available at: www.gov.uk/government/publications/disqualification-under-the-childcare-act-2006 . Other providers may also find it helpful to refer to this guidance.

suitability of any person who is in regular contact with children on the premises where childcare is provided. The disqualification of an employee could be an instance of a significant event.

3.17 The registered provider must give Ofsted or the childminder agency with which they are registered, the following information about themselves or about any person who lives in the same household as the registered provider or who is employed in the household:

- details of any order, determination, conviction, or other ground for disqualification from registration under regulations made under section 75 of the Childcare Act 2006
- the date of the order, determination or conviction, or the date when the other ground for disqualification arose
- the body or court which made the order, determination or conviction, and the sentence (if any) imposed
- a certified copy of the relevant order (in relation to an order or conviction)

3.18 The information must be provided to Ofsted or the childminder agency with which they are registered as soon as reasonably practicable, but at the latest within 14 days of the date the provider became aware of the information or ought reasonably to have become aware of it if they had made reasonable enquiries[29].

Staff taking medication/other substances

3.19 Staff members must not be under the influence of alcohol or any other substance which may affect their ability to care for children. If a staff member is taking medication which may affect their ability to care for children, the staff member should seek medical advice. Providers must ensure that staff members only work directly with children if medical advice confirms that the medication is unlikely to impair that staff member's ability to look after children properly. All medication on the premises must be securely stored, and out of reach of children, at all times.

Staff qualifications, training, support and skills

3.20 Providers must follow their legal responsibilities under the Equality Act 2010 including the fair and equal treatment of practitioners regardless of age, disability, gender reassignment, marriage and civil partnership, pregnancy and maternity, race, religion or belief, sex and sexual orientation.

3.21 The daily experience of children in early years settings and the overall quality of provision depends on all practitioners having appropriate qualifications, training, skills, knowledge, and a clear understanding of their roles and responsibilities. Providers must ensure that all staff receive induction training to help them understand their roles and responsibilities. Induction training must include information about emergency evacuation procedures, safeguarding, child protection, and

---

[29]This requirement is set out in Regulation 12 of The Childcare (Disqualification) and Childcare (Early Years Provision Free of Charge) (Extended Entitlement) (Amendment) Regulations 2018. (S.I. 2018/794)

health and safety issues. Providers must support staff to undertake appropriate training and professional development opportunities to ensure they offer quality learning and development experiences for children that continually improves.

3.22   Providers must put appropriate arrangements in place for the supervision of staff who have contact with children and families. Effective supervision provides support, coaching and training for the practitioner and promotes the interests of children. Supervision should foster a culture of mutual support, teamwork and continuous improvement, which encourages the confidential discussion of sensitive issues.

3.23   Supervision should provide opportunities for staff to:

- discuss any issues – particularly concerning children's development or well-being, including child protection concerns
- identify solutions to address issues as they arise
- receive coaching to improve their personal effectiveness

3.24   Childminders must have completed training which helps them to understand and implement the EYFS before they can register with Ofsted or a childminder agency. Childminders are accountable for the quality of the work of any assistants, and must be satisfied that assistants are competent in the areas of work they undertake.

3.25   At least one person who has a current paediatric first aid (PFA) certificate must be on the premises and available at all times when children are present, and must accompany children on outings. The certificate must be for a full course consistent with the criteria set out in Annex A. Childminders, and any assistant who might be in sole charge of the children for any period of time, must hold a full current PFA certificate. PFA training[30] must be renewed every three years and be relevant for workers caring for young children and where relevant, babies. Providers should take into account the number of children, staff and layout of premises to ensure that a paediatric first aider is able to respond to emergencies quickly. All newly qualified[31] entrants to the early years workforce who have completed a level 2 and/or level 3 qualification on or after 30 June 2016, must also have either a full PFA or an emergency PFA certificate within three months of starting work in order to be included in the required staff:child ratios at level 2 or level 3 in an early

---

[30]Providers are responsible for identifying and selecting a competent training provider to deliver their PFA training. Training is available from a wide range of providers including: those who offer regulated qualifications; or the Voluntary Aid Societies (St John Ambulance, the British Red Cross and St Andrew's First Aid who together are acknowledged by the Health and Safety Executive (HSE) as one of the standard-setters for currently accepted first aid practice for first aid at work training courses); or those who operate under voluntary accreditation schemes; or one that is a member of a trade body with an approval and monitoring scheme; or those who operate independently of any such accreditation scheme. The Register of Regulated Qualifications may help providers identify PFA providers, which can be found at: http://register.ofqual.gov.uk/qualification. It may also be helpful to refer to HSE's guidance about choosing a first aid training provider, which can be found at: www.hse.gov.uk/pubns/geis3.htm

[31]In this context, "newly qualified entrants" includes staff who have been apprentices or long term students who have gained a level 2 or level 3 early years qualification.

years setting[32]. Providers should display (or make available to parents) staff PFA certificates or a list of staff who have a current PFA certificate.

3.26   Providers must ensure that staff have sufficient understanding and use of English to ensure the well-being of children in their care. For example, settings must be in a position to keep records in English, to liaise with other agencies in English, to summon emergency help, and to understand instructions such as those for the safety of medicines or food hygiene.

Key person

3.27   Each child must be assigned a key person. Their role is to help ensure that every child's care is tailored to meet their individual needs (in accordance with paragraph 1.16), to help the child become familiar with the setting, offer a settled relationship for the child and build a relationship with their parents.

Staff:child ratios – all providers (including childminders)

3.28   In settings on the early years register, the manager must hold an approved[33] level 3[34] qualification or above and at least half of all other staff must hold at least an approved level 2 qualification[35]. The manager should have at least two years' experience of working in an early years setting, or have at least two years' other suitable experience. The provider must ensure there is a named deputy who, in their judgement, is capable and qualified[36] to take charge in the manager's absence.

3.29   Staffing arrangements must meet the needs of all children and ensure their safety. Providers must ensure that children are adequately supervised, including whilst eating, and decide how to deploy staff to ensure children's needs are met. Providers must inform parents and/or carers about staff deployment, and, when relevant and practical, aim to involve them in these decisions. Children must usually be within sight and hearing of staff and always within sight or hearing.

---

[32]Providers can make an exception to this requirement where a newly qualified entrant to the workforce is unable to gain a PFA certificate if a disability would prevent them from doing so. Such a newly qualified entrant can still be included in the staff:child ratios if otherwise competent to carry out their childcare duties. Where possible, such staff should attend a relevant PFA training course and obtain written evidence of attendance.

[33]As defined by the Department for Education on the Early Years Qualifications List published on GOV. UK: https://www.gov.uk/guidance/early-years-qualifications-finder which also includes information on overseas qualifications.

[34]To count in the ratios at level 3, staff holding an Early Years Educator qualification must also have achieved a suitable level 2 qualification in English and maths as defined by the Department for Education on the Early Years Qualifications List published on GOV.UK: https://www.gov.uk/guidance/early-years-qualifications-finder

[35]These qualification requirements do not apply to out-of-school provision for reception aged children, (see paragraph 3.41), and/or childminders.

[36]'Capable and qualified' includes having necessary skills and knowledge to deputise. A deputy does not have to have any specific qualification.

3.30   Only those aged 17 or over may be included in ratios if they are suitable, as in paragraphs 3.9 to 3.11 (and staff under 17 should be supervised at all times). Suitable students on long term placements and volunteers (aged 17 or over) and staff working as apprentices in early education (aged 16 or over) may be included in the ratios if the provider is satisfied that they are competent and responsible.

3.31   The ratio and qualification requirements below apply to the total number of staff available to work directly with children[37]. Exceptionally, and where the quality of care and safety and security of children is maintained, changes to the ratios may be made. This applies to all settings but childminders cannot have more than six children under the age of eight per adult providing care. For group settings providing overnight care, the relevant ratios continue to apply and at least one member of staff must be awake at all times.

Early years providers (other than childminders)

3.32   For children aged under two:

- there must be at least one member of staff for every three children
- at least one member of staff must hold an approved level 3 qualification, and must be suitably experienced in working with children under two
- at least half of all other staff must hold an approved level 2 qualification
- at least half of all staff must have received training that specifically addresses the care of babies
- where there is a room for under two-year-olds, the member of staff in charge of that room must, in the judgement of the provider, have suitable experience of working with under twos

3.33   For children aged two:

- there must be at least one member of staff for every four children[38]
- at least one member of staff must hold an approved level 3 qualification
- at least half of all other staff must hold an approved level 2 qualification

3.34   For children aged three and over in registered early years provision where a person with Qualified Teacher Status, Early Years Professional Status, Early Years Teacher Status or another approved level 6 qualification, is working directly with the children[39]:

---

[37]Ofsted may determine that providers must observe a higher staff:child ratio than outlined here to ensure the safety and welfare of children.

[38]In a maintained school or non-maintained special school, where the two-year-olds are pupils, staff must additionally be under the direction and supervision of a qualified or nominated teacher when carrying out specified work (as laid out in the Education (Specified Work) (England) Regulations 2012). Specified work broadly encompasses lesson (or curriculum) planning, delivering lessons, assessing the development, progress and attainment of pupils and reporting on the latter. The headteacher must be satisfied that the staff have the skills, expertise and experience needed to carry out the work and determine the appropriate level of direction and supervision.

[39]We expect the teacher (or equivalent) to be working with children for the vast majority of the time. Where they need to be absent for short periods of time, the provider will need to ensure that quality and safety is maintained.

- there must be at least one member of staff for every 13 children
- at least one other member of staff must hold an approved level 3 qualification

3.35   For children aged three and over at any time in registered early years provision when a person with Qualified Teacher Status, Early Years Professional Status, Early Years Teacher Status or another approved level 6 qualification is not working directly with the children:

- there must be at least one member of staff for every eight children
- at least one member of staff must hold an approved level 3 qualification
- at least half of all other staff must hold an approved level 2 qualification

3.36   For children aged three and over in independent schools (including in nursery classes in free schools and academies), where a person with Qualified Teacher Status, Early Years Professional Status, Early Years Teacher Status or another approved level 6 qualification, an instructor[40], or another suitably qualified overseas trained teacher, is working directly with the children:

- for classes where the majority of children will reach the age of five or older within the school year, there must be at least one member of staff for every 30 children[41]
- for all other classes there must be at least one member of staff for every 13 children
- at least one other member of staff must hold an approved level 3 qualification

3.37   For children aged three and over in independent schools (including in nursery classes in academies), where there is no person with Qualified Teacher Status, Early Years Professional Status, Early Years Teacher Status or another approved level 6 qualification, no instructor, and no suitably qualified overseas trained teacher, working directly with the children:

- there must be at least one member of staff for every eight children
- at least one member of staff must hold an approved level 3 qualification
- at least half of all other staff must hold an approved level 2 qualification

3.38   For children aged three and over in maintained nursery schools and nursery classes in maintained schools[42]:

---

[40]An instructor is a person at the school who provides education which consists of instruction in any art or skill, or in any subject or group of subjects, in circumstances where: (a) special qualifications or experience or both are required for such instruction; and (b) the person or body of persons responsible for the management of the school is satisfied as to the qualifications or experience (or both) of the person providing education.

[41]Subject to any permitted exceptions under The Schools Admissions (Infant Class Sizes) Regulations 2012 S.I. 2012/10.

[42]Where schools have provision run by the governing body (under section 27 of the Education Act 2002) for three- and four-year-olds who are not pupils of the school, they can apply: a 1:13 ratio where a person with a suitable level 6 qualification is working directly with the children (as in paragraph 3.34); or a 1:8 ratio where a person with a suitable level 6 qualification is not working directly with children but at least one member of staff present holds a level 3 qualification (as in paragraph 3.35).

- there must be at least one member of staff for every 13 children[43]
- at least one member of staff must be a school teacher as defined by section 122 of the Education Act 2002[44]
- at least one other member of staff must hold an approved level 3 qualification[45]

3.39 Reception classes in maintained schools and academies are subject to infant class size legislation.[46] The School Admissions (Infant Class Size) Regulations 2012 limit the size of infant classes to 30 pupils per school teacher[47] (subject to permitted exceptions) while an ordinary teaching session is conducted. 'School teachers' do not include teaching assistants, higher level teaching assistants or other support staff. Consequently, in an ordinary teaching session, a school must employ sufficient school teachers to enable it to teach its infant classes in groups of no more than 30 per school teacher[48].

3.40 Some schools may choose to mix their reception classes with groups of younger children (nursery pupils, non pupils or younger children from a registered provider), in which case they must determine ratios within mixed groups, guided by all relevant ratio requirements and by the needs of individual children within the group. In exercising this discretion, the school must comply with the statutory requirements relating to the education of children of compulsory school age and infant class sizes. Schools' partner providers must meet the relevant ratio requirements for their provision.

Before/after school care and holiday provision

3.41 Where the provision is solely before/after school[49] care or holiday provision for children who normally attend reception class (or older) during the school day, there must be sufficient staff as for a class of 30 children. It is for providers to determine how many staff are needed to ensure the safety and welfare of children, bearing in mind the type(s) of activity and the age and needs of the children. It is also for providers to determine what qualifications, if any,

---

[43]Where children in nursery classes attend school for longer than the school day or in the school holidays, in provision run directly by the governing body or the proprietor, with no teacher present, a ratio of one member of staff to every eight children can be applied if at least one member of staff holds a full and relevant level 3 qualification, and at least half of all other staff hold a full and relevant level 2 qualification.

[44]See also the Education (School Teachers' Prescribed Qualifications, etc) Order 2003 and the Education (School Teachers' Qualifications) (England) Regulations 2003.

[45]Provided that the person meets all relevant staff qualification requirement as required by The School Staffing (England) Regulations 2009.

[46]Academies are required by their funding agreements to comply with the School Admissions Code and the law relating to admissions although the Secretary of State has the power to vary this requirement where there is demonstratable need.

[47]As defined by section 122 of the Education Act 2002.

[48]The Specified Work Regulations 2012 allow a non-teacher to carry out the work of the teacher ("specified work") where the non-teacher is assisting or supporting the work of the teacher, is subject to the teacher's direction and supervision as arranged with the headteacher, and the headteacher is satisfied that that person has the skills, expertise and experience required to carry out the specified work. In an academy a teacher can have whatever qualification the trust regard as appropriate to teach an infant class, in line with admissions law.

[49]'School' means maintained schools, non-maintained schools, independent schools and academies.

the manager and/or staff should have. See footnote 5 at paragraph 1.1 for the learning and development requirements for providers offering care exclusively before/after school or during the school holidays.

Childminders

3.42   At any one time, childminders (whether providing the childminding on domestic or non-domestic premises) may care for a maximum of six children under the age of eight[50].

3.43   If a childminder can demonstrate to parents and/or carers and Ofsted inspectors or their childminder agency that the individual needs of all the children are being met, exceptions to the usual ratios can be made for example:

- when childminders are caring for sibling babies, or
- when caring for their own baby, or
- to maintain continuity of care, or
- if children aged three to five only attend the childminding setting before and/or after a normal school day[51], and/or during school holidays, they may be cared for at the same time as three other young children.

In all circumstances, the total number of children under the age of eight being cared for must not exceed six per adult.

3.44   If a childminder employs an assistant or works with another childminder, each childminder (or assistant) may care for the number of children permitted by the ratios specified above[52]. Children may be left in the sole care of childminders' assistants for two hours at most in a single day[53]. Childminders must obtain parents and/or carers' permission to leave children with an assistant, including for very short periods of time. For childminders providing overnight care, the ratios continue to apply and the childminder must always be able to hear the children (this may be via a monitor).

Health

Medicines

3.45   The provider must promote the good health, including the oral health, of children attending the setting. They must have a procedure, discussed with parents and/or carers, for responding to children who are ill or infectious, take necessary steps to prevent the spread of infection, and take appropriate action if children are ill[54].

---

[50]Including the childminder's own children or any other children for whom they are responsible such as those being fostered.

[51]Can be defined as 9 am to 3 pm or the normal full day applicable to the school the child attends.

[52]Subject to any restrictions imposed by Ofsted or the relevant childminder agency on registration.

[53]The Childcare (Exemptions from Registration) Order 2008 specifies that where provision is made for a particular child for two hours or less a day, the carer is exempt from registration as a childminder.

[54]Guidance on health protection in schools and other childcare facilities which sets out when and for how long children need to be excluded from settings, when treatment/medication is required and where to get further advice can be found at https://www.gov.uk/government/publications/health-protection-in-schools-and-other-childcare-facilities

3.46 Providers must have and implement a policy, and procedures, for administering medicines. It must include systems for obtaining information about a child's needs for medicines, and for keeping this information up-to-date. Training must be provided for staff where the administration of medicine requires medical or technical knowledge. Prescription medicines must not be administered unless they have been prescribed for a child by a doctor, dentist, nurse or pharmacist (medicines containing aspirin should only be given if prescribed by a doctor).

3.47 Medicine (both prescription and non-prescription[55]) must only be administered to a child where written permission for that particular medicine has been obtained from the child's parent and/or carer. Providers must keep a written record each time a medicine is administered to a child, and inform the child's parents and/or carers on the same day, or as soon as reasonably practicable.

Food and drink

3.48 Where children are provided with meals, snacks and drinks, they must be healthy, balanced and nutritious[56]. Before a child is admitted to the setting the provider must also obtain information about any special dietary requirements, preferences and food allergies that the child has, and any special health requirements. Fresh drinking water must be available and accessible to children at all times. Providers must record and act on information from parents and carers about a child's dietary needs.

3.49 There must be an area which is adequately equipped to provide healthy meals, snacks and drinks for children as necessary. There must be suitable facilities for the hygienic preparation of food for children, if necessary including suitable sterilisation equipment for babies' food. Providers must be confident that those responsible for preparing and handling food are competent to do so. In group provision, all staff involved in preparing and handling food must receive training in food hygiene. In addition, section 4 of 'Example menus for early years settings in England' (see footnote 56) includes guidance on menu planning, food safety, managing food allergies and reading food labels, which staff preparing food will find helpful in ensuring that children are kept safe.

3.50 Registered providers must notify Ofsted or the childminder agency with which they are registered of any food poisoning affecting two or more children cared for on the premises. Notification must be made as soon as is reasonably practicable, but in any event within 14 days of the incident.

---

[55]Non-prescription medicines can include those that can be purchased from pharmacies (including some over the counter medicines which can only be purchased from a pharmacy), health shops and supermarkets. See also BMA advice: https://www.bma.org.uk/advice-and-support/gp-practices/managing-workload/prescribing-over-the-counter-medicines-in-nurseries-and-schools

[56]For example menus and guidance see: https://www.gov.uk/government/publications/example-menus-for-early-years-settings-in-england.

A registered provider, who, without reasonable excuse, fails to comply with this requirement, commits an offence.

Accident or injury

3.51   Providers must ensure there is a first aid box accessible at all times with appropriate content for use with children. Providers must keep a written record of accidents or injuries and first aid treatment. Providers must inform parents and/or carers of any accident or injury sustained by the child on the same day as, or as soon as reasonably practicable after, and of any first aid treatment given.

3.52   Registered providers must notify Ofsted or the childminder agency with which they are registered of any serious accident, illness or injury to, or death of, any child while in their care, and of the action taken. Notification must be made as soon as is reasonably practicable, but in any event within 14 days of the incident occurring. A registered provider, who, without reasonable excuse, fails to comply with this requirement, commits an offence. Providers must notify local child protection agencies of any serious accident or injury to, or the death of, any child while in their care, and must act on any advice from those agencies.

Managing children's behaviour

3.53   Providers are responsible for managing children's behaviour in an appropriate way.

3.54   Providers must not give or threaten corporal punishment to a child and must not use or threaten any punishment which could adversely affect a child's well-being. Providers must take all reasonable steps to ensure that corporal punishment is not given by any person who cares for or is in regular contact with a child, or by any person living or working in the premises where care is provided. Any early years provider who fails to meet these requirements commits an offence. A person will not be taken to have used corporal punishment (and therefore will not have committed an offence), where physical intervention[57] was taken for the purposes of averting immediate danger of personal injury to any person (including the child) or to manage a child's behaviour if absolutely necessary. Providers, including childminders, must keep a record of any occasion where physical intervention is used, and parents and/or carers must be informed on the same day, or as soon as reasonably practicable.

---

[57]Physical intervention is where practitioners use reasonable force to prevent children from injuring themselves or others or damaging property.

Safety and suitability of premises, environment and equipment

Safety

3.55   Providers must ensure that their premises, including overall floor space and outdoor spaces, are fit for purpose and suitable for the age of children cared for and the activities provided on the premises. Providers must comply with requirements of health and safety legislation (including fire safety and hygiene requirements).

3.56   Providers must take reasonable steps to ensure the safety of children, staff and others on the premises in the case of fire or any other emergency, and must have an emergency evacuation procedure. Providers must have appropriate fire detection and control equipment (for example, fire alarms, smoke detectors, fire blankets and/or fire extinguishers) which is in working order. Fire exits must be clearly identifiable, and fire doors must be free of obstruction and easily opened from the inside.

Smoking and Vaping

3.57   Providers must not allow smoking in or on the premises when children are present or about to be present. Staff should not vape or use e-cigarettes when children are present and providers should consider Public Health England advice on their use in public places and workplaces[58].

Premises

3.58   The premises and equipment must be organised in a way that meets the needs of children. Providers must meet the following indoor space requirements[59] where indoor activity in a building(s) forms the main part of (or is integral) to the provision:

- Children under two years: 3.5 m² per child
- Two year olds: 2.5 m² per child
- Children aged three to five years: 2.3 m² per child

Where the space standards are applied, providers cannot increase the number of children on roll because they additionally use an outside area. Forest and other exclusively (or almost exclusively) outdoor provision is not required to meet the space standards above as long as children's needs can be met. For this kind of provision, indoor space requirements can be used as a guide for the minimum area needed.

[58]Public Health England advice in 'Use of e-cigarettes in public places and workplaces' can be found at https://www.gov.uk/government/publications/use-of-e-cigarettes-in-public-places-and-workplaces

[59]These calculations should be based on the net or useable areas of the rooms used by the children, not including storage areas, thoroughfares, dedicated staff areas, cloakrooms, utility rooms, kitchens and toilets.

3.59   Providers must provide access to an outdoor play area or, if that is not pos-sible, ensure that outdoor activities are planned and taken on a daily basis (unless circumstances make this inappropriate, for example unsafe weather conditions). Providers must follow their legal responsibilities under the Equality Act 2010 (for example, the provisions on reasonable adjustments).

3.60   Sleeping children must be frequently checked to ensure that they are safe[60]. Being safe includes ensuring that cots/bedding are in good condition and suited to the age of the child, and that infants are placed down to sleep safely in line with latest government safety guidance[61]. Except in childmind-ing settings, there should be a separate baby room for children under the age of two. However, providers must ensure that children in a baby room have contact with older children and are moved into the older age group when appropriate.

3.61   Providers must ensure there is an adequate number of toilets and hand basins available. Except in childminding settings, there should usually be separate toilet facilities for adults. Providers must ensure there are suitable hygienic changing facilities for changing any children who are in nappies and providers should ensure that an adequate supply of clean bedding, tow-els, spare clothes and any other necessary items is always available.

3.62   Providers must also ensure that there is an area where staff may talk to par-ents and/or carers confidentially, as well as an area in group settings for staff to take breaks away from areas being used by children.

3.63   Providers must only release children into the care of individuals who have been notified to the provider by the parent, and must ensure that children do not leave the premises unsupervised. Providers must take all reasonable steps to prevent unauthorised persons entering the premises[62], and have an agreed procedure for checking the identity of visitors. Providers must con-sider what additional measures are necessary when children stay overnight.

3.64   Providers must carry the appropriate insurance (e.g. public liability insurance) to cover all premises from which they provide childcare or childminding.

Risk assessment

3.65   Providers must ensure that they take all reasonable steps to ensure staff and children in their care are not exposed to risks and must be able to demonstrate

---

[60]NHS advice on Sudden Infant Death Syndrome: https://www.nhs.uk/conditions/sudden-infant-death-syndrome-sids/

[61]Providers may find it helpful to refer to NHS advice for further information on safety of sleeping children: 'https://www.nhs.uk/conditions/baby/caring-for-a-newborn/reduce-the-risk-of-sudden-infant-death-syndrome/

[62]Where childminders are operating out of non-domestic premises which are routinely accessed by members of the public (e.g. a hotel or a community centre), childminders must take all reasonable steps to prevent unauthorised persons entering the part of those premises in which the children are being cared for.

how they are managing risks[63]. Providers must determine where it is helpful to make some written risk assessments in relation to specific issues, to inform staff practice, and to demonstrate how they are managing risks if asked by parents and/or carers or inspectors. Risk assessments should identify aspects of the environment that need to be checked on a regular basis, when and by whom those aspects will be checked, and how the risk will be removed or minimised.

Outings

3.66   Children must be kept safe while on outings. Providers must assess the risks or hazards which may arise for the children, and must identify the steps to be taken to remove, minimise and manage those risks and hazards. The assessment must include consideration of adult to child ratios. The risk assessment does not necessarily need to be in writing; this is for providers to judge.

3.67   Vehicles in which children are being transported, and the driver of those vehicles, must be adequately insured.

Special educational needs

3.68   Providers must have arrangements in place to support children with SEN or disabilities. Maintained schools, maintained nursery schools and all providers who are funded by the local authority to deliver early education places must have regard to the Special Educational Needs Code of Practice[64]. Maintained schools and maintained nursery schools must identify a member of staff to act as Special Educational Needs Co-ordinator (SENCO) and other providers (in group provision) are expected to identify a SENCO. Childminders are encouraged to identify a person to act as a SENCO and childminders who are registered with a childminder agency or who are part of a network may wish to share the role between them.

---

[63]Guidance on risk assessments, including where written ones may be required where five or more staff are employed, can be obtained from the Health and Safety Executive. https://www.hse.gov.uk/simple-health-safety/risk/index.htm

[64]www.gov.uk/government/publications/send-code-of-practice-0-to-25

Information and records

3.69 Providers must maintain records and obtain and share information (with parents and carers, other professionals working with the child, the police, social services and Ofsted or the childminder agency with which they are registered, as appropriate) to ensure the safe and efficient management of the setting, and to help ensure the needs of all children are met[65]. Providers must enable a regular two-way flow of information with parents and/or carers, and between providers, if a child is attending more than one setting. If requested, providers should incorporate parents' and/or carers' comments into children's records.

3.70 Records must be easily accessible and available (these may be kept securely off the premises). Confidential information and records about staff and children must be held securely and only accessible and available to those who have a right or professional need to see them[66]. Providers must be aware of their responsibilities under the Data Protection Legislation[67] and where relevant the Freedom of Information Act 2000.

3.71 Providers must ensure that all staff understand the need to protect the privacy of the children in their care as well the legal requirements that exist to ensure that information relating to the child is handled in a way that ensures confidentiality. Parents and/or carers must be given access to all records about their child, provided that no relevant exemptions apply to their disclosure under the Data Protection Act[68].

3.72 Records relating to individual children must be retained for a reasonable period of time after they have left the provision[69].

Information about the child

3.73 Providers must record the following information for each child in their care: full name; date of birth; name and address of every parent and/or carer who is known to the provider (and information about any other person who has parental responsibility for the child); which parent(s) and/or carer(s) the child normally lives with; and emergency contact details for parents and/or carers.

---

[65]Guidance on sharing information with relevant services when there are safeguarding concerns is available via: https://www.gov.uk/government/publications/safeguarding-practitioners-information-sharing-advice

[66]The National Cyber Security Centre (NCSC) has published helpful guidance on cyber security: https://www.ncsc.gov.uk/guidance/early-years-practitioners-using-cyber-security-to-protect-your-settings

[67]This includes the Data Protection Act 2018 and General Data Protection Regulation 2018 see: https://www.gov.uk/government/publications/guide-to-the-general-data-protection-regulation.

[68]The Data Protection Act 2018 (DPA) gives parents and carers the right to access information about their child that a provider holds. However, the DPA also sets out specific exemptions under which certain personal information may, under specific circumstances, be withheld from release. For example, a relevant professional will need to give careful consideration as to whether the disclosure of certain information about a child could cause harm either to the child or any other individual. It is therefore essential that all providers/staff in early years settings have an understanding of how data protection laws operate. Further guidance can be found on the website of the Information Commissioner's Office at: https://ico.org.uk/for-organisations/guide-to-the-general-data-protection-regulation-gdpr/

[69]Individual providers should determine how long to retain records relating to individual children.

Information for parents and carers

3.74   Providers must make the following information available to parents and/or carers:

- how the EYFS is being delivered in the setting, and how parents and/or carers can access more information
- the range and type of activities and experiences provided for children, the daily routines of the setting, and how parents and carers can share learning at home
- how the setting supports children with special educational needs and disabilities
- food and drinks provided for children
- details of the provider's policies and procedures (all providers except childminders (see paragraph 3.3) must make copies available on request) including the procedure to be followed in the event of a parent and/or carer failing to collect a child at the appointed time, or in the event of a child going missing at, or away from, the setting
- staffing in the setting; the name of their child's key person and their role; and a telephone number for parents and/or carers to contact in an emergency

Complaints

3.75   Providers must put in place a written procedure for dealing with concerns and complaints from parents and/or carers, and must keep a written record of any complaints, and their outcome. Childminders are not required to have a written procedure for handling complaints, but they must keep a record of any complaints they receive and their outcome. All providers must investigate written complaints relating to their fulfilment of the EYFS requirements and notify complainants of the outcome of the investigation within 28 days of having received the complaint. The record of complaints must be made available to Ofsted or the relevant childminder agency on request.

3.76   Providers must make available to parents and/or carers details about how to contact Ofsted or the childminder agency with which the provider is registered as appropriate, if they believe the provider is not meeting the EYFS requirements. If providers become aware that they are to be inspected by Ofsted or have a quality assurance visit by the childminder agency, they must notify parents and/or carers. After an inspection by Ofsted or a quality assurance visit by their childminder agency, providers must supply a copy of the report to parents and/or carers of children attending on a regular basis.

Information about the provider

3.77   Providers must hold the following documentation:

- name, home address and telephone number of the provider and any other person living or employed on the premises (this requirement does not apply to childminders)
- name, home address and telephone number of anyone else who will regularly be in unsupervised contact with the children attending the early years provision

- a daily record of the names of the children being cared for on the premises, their hours of attendance and the names of each child's key person
- their certificate of registration (which must be displayed at the setting and shown to parents and/or carers on request)

Changes that must be notified to Ofsted or the relevant childminder agency (CMA)

3.78   All registered early years providers must notify Ofsted or the CMA with which they are registered of any change:

- in the address of the premises (and seek approval to operate from those premises where appropriate); to the premises which may affect the space available to children and the quality of childcare available to them; in the name or address of the provider, or the provider's other contact information; to the person who is managing the early years provision; in the persons aged 16 years or older living or working on any domestic premises from which childminding is provided; or to the persons caring for children on any premises where childminding is provided[70]
- any proposal to change the hours during which childcare is provided; or to provide overnight care
- any significant event which is likely to affect the suitability of the early years provider or any person who cares for, or is in regular contact with, children on the premises to look after children
- where the early years provision is provided by a company, any change in the name or registered number of the company
- where the early years provision is provided by a charity, any change in the name or registration number of the charity
- where the childcare is provided by a partnership, body corporate or unincorporated association, any change to the 'nominated individual'
- where the childcare is provided by a partnership, body corporate or unincorporated association whose sole or main purpose is the provision of childcare, any change to the individuals who are partners in, or a director, secretary or other officer or members of its governing body

3.79   Where providers are required to notify Ofsted or their CMA about a change of person except for managers, as specified in paragraph 3.78 above, providers must give Ofsted or their CMA the new person's name, any former names or aliases, date of birth, and home address. If there is a change of manager, providers must notify Ofsted or their CMA that a new manager has been appointed. Where it is reasonably practicable to do so, notification must be made in advance. In other cases, notification must be made as soon as is reasonably practicable, but always within 14 days. A registered provider who, without reasonable excuse, fails to comply with these requirements commits an offence.

---

[70]A person is not considered to be working on the premises if none of their work is done in the part of the premises in which children are cared for, or if they do not work on the premises at times when children are there.

Other Legal Duties

3.80   The EYFS requirements sit alongside other legal obligations and do not supersede or replace any other legislation which providers must still meet. For example, where provision is taking place in maintained schools there is other legislation in place with which headteachers, teachers and other practitioners must comply with. Other duties on providers include:

- employment laws;
- anti-discriminatory legislation;
- health and safety legislation;
- data collection regulations;
- duty of care.

ANNEX A

CRITERIA FOR EFFECTIVE PAEDIATRIC FIRST AID (PFA) TRAINING

1. Training is designed for workers caring for young children in the absence of their parents and is appropriate to the age of the children being cared for.
2. Following training an assessment of competence leads to the award of a certificate.
3. The certificate must be renewed every three years.
4. Adequate resuscitation and other equipment including baby and junior models must be provided, so that all trainees are able to practice and demonstrate techniques.
5. The **emergency PFA** course should be undertaken face-to-face[71] and last for a minimum of 6 hours (excluding breaks) and cover the following areas:

   - Be able to assess an emergency situation and prioritise what action to take
   - Help a baby or child who is unresponsive and breathing normally
   - Help a baby or child who is unresponsive and not breathing normally
   - Help a baby or child who is having a seizure
   - Help a baby or child who is choking
   - Help a baby or child who is bleeding
   - Help a baby or child who is suffering from shock caused by severe blood loss (hypovolemic shock)

6. The **full PFA** course should last for a minimum of 12 hours (excluding breaks) and cover the elements listed below in addition to the areas set out in paragraph 5 (the emergency PFA training elements outlined in paragraph 5 should be delivered face to face).

   - Help a baby or child who is suffering from anaphylactic shock
   - Help a baby or child who has had an electric shock
   - Help a baby or child who has burns or scalds
   - Help a baby or child who has a suspected fracture
   - Help a baby or child with head, neck or back injuries
   - Help a baby or child who is suspected of being poisoned
   - Help a baby or child with a foreign body in eyes, ears or nose
   - Help a baby or child with an eye injury
   - Help a baby or child with a bite or sting
   - Help a baby or child who is suffering from the effects of extreme heat or cold

---

[71]Face to face means trainers are physically present with their trainees. This excludes the use of online platforms.

- Help a baby or child having: a diabetic emergency; an asthma attack; an allergic reaction; meningitis; and/or febrile convulsions
- Understand the role and responsibilities of the paediatric first aider (including appropriate contents of a first aid box and the need for recording accidents and incidents)

7. Providers should consider whether paediatric first aiders need to undertake annual refresher training, during any three year certification period to help maintain basic skills and keep up to date with any changes to PFA procedures.

ANNEX B

STATUTORY GUIDANCE FOR THE RECEPTION
BASELINE ASSESSMENT

CONTENTS

SUMMARY

About this guidance

This is statutory guidance from the Department for Education. This means that recipients must have regard to it when administering Reception Baseline Assessments (RBAs). This guidance covers all intakes in reception within an academic year including during autumn, spring and summer terms from that date.

The statutory requirements in this annex are indicated by the use of the word "must". Additionally, providers must "have regard" to other provisions in these sections. These provisions are indicated by the use of the word "should". "Having regard" to these provisions means that practitioners must take them into account when completing the Reception Baseline Assessment (RBA) and should not depart from them unless there is good reason for doing so.

Review date

This guidance will be reviewed on a rolling basis and will remain in force until further notice.

Further guidance on assessment and reporting arrangements for the RBA is published annually. Schools must administer the assessment in accordance with administration guidance and the assessment and reporting arrangements.

What legislation does this guidance refer to?

- the Childcare Act 2006
- the Early Years Foundation Stage (Learning and Development Requirements) Order 2007 underpins the requirement for schools to administer the RBA. This has been amended to ensure the assessment is included in these requirements on a statutory basis.

Who is this guidance for?

This guidance is for:

- school leaders, school staff and governing bodies in all maintained schools, academies and free schools with a reception cohort
- this guidance does not apply to independent schools, or pupil referral units (PRUs).
- this guidance does not apply to nurseries, childminders or schools without a reception cohort.

INTRODUCTION AND PURPOSE

The RBA is a short assessment, taken in the first six weeks in which a child starts reception.

Accountability and Progress

1. The RBA assesses a child in early mathematics, literacy, communication and language. The purpose of the RBA is to form the starting point for cohort-level school progress measures. Data from the RBA is compared to key stage 2 outcomes 7 years later to form the overall progress measure for a school.

2. The RBA is not used to make judgements about early years provision, either current or retrospective. It is solely intended for use within the primary school progress measure.

Assessment Data

3. The RBA and its data should not be used for any other purpose apart from the progress measure. Data collected and produced from the assessment will be stored in the National Pupil Database (NPD). The data, including numerical scores, is not shared with external bodies, including schools, teachers, pupils or parents/carers.

4. The RBA is not suitable as a formative or diagnostic assessment. Scores are not shared or published to prevent any labelling and streaming of children or judgement of early years providers. Instead, teachers receive a series of narrative statements informing them of how the child performed on the day. There is no expected standard and children cannot pass or fail.

ASSESSMENT ADMINISTRATION

Timing

5. Schools have a window of six weeks in which they can administer the assessment, commencing as soon as each child starts reception. The six week period applies for autumn, winter and summer intakes, or any pupil that joins a school mid-term and hasn't previously taken the RBA.
6. The assessment can be carried out at any time within those six weeks, within the school day. The assessment must be administered within this window. The RBA does not have to be completed in one sitting and practitioners may pause the assessment at any time they feel is appropriate.

Administration of the RBA

7. Schools must administer the assessment in accordance with administration guidance and assessment and reporting arrangements published annually.
8. The RBA is a short, interactive assessment. Although the assessment is not timed, it has been designed to take around 20 minutes. The assessment can be carried out by a teacher, teaching assistant, early years practitioner or any other trained education professional who should be familiar with the child taking the assessment.

Security of Assessment Materials

9. Headteachers must ensure that confidentiality of assessment materials is maintained so that no child has an unfair advantage. Schools must follow guidance on how to keep materials secure and treat them as confidential when they are received.
10. Assessment materials must not be used for any other purpose but for delivering the assessment.

INCLUSION AND PARTICIPATION

Schools for Inclusion

11. All maintained schools and academies with a reception cohort will be required to participate in the assessment. This includes, but is not limited to, Service Children Education (SCE) schools, infant and first schools and special schools. The RBA is to be administered to all pupils registered in a reception class in the schools specified.

12. The reception to key stage 2 progress measure will be applicable to the vast majority of schools in the primary phase – those where pupils enter in reception and leave in year 6. Other school types – infant, first, junior and middle schools – will be expected to ensure their pupils' make good progress and, like all schools, to be able to explain to Ofsted how they have planned and implemented their curriculum and what impact that is having for pupils. KS2 attainment information will continue to be available for middle and junior schools.

13. Independent schools and nurseries, childminders, Pupil Referral Units (PRUs) and early years or primary school settings without a reception cohort, including maintained and voluntary nurseries and junior schools, are exempt from participation in the assessment.

Pupils for Inclusion

14. All assessments are required to meet Ofqual's regulatory framework[72] which states 'assessment should minimise bias, differentiating only on the basis of each pupil's level of attainment. A pupil should not be disadvantaged by factors that do not relate to what is being tested.'

15. The RBA has been developed to be an inclusive assessment, accessible to the majority of pupils on entry to school. It has been designed so that pupils with SEND and those learning English as an additional language can participate.

16. Modified resources are available for pupils with visual and hearing impairments and practitioners should also consider making further adaptations for those who require it, such as copying resources onto coloured paper or enlarging some resources to a size appropriate to pupils. Headteachers must ensure that the confidentiality of the assessment is maintained while any modifications are being made.

17. In some rare cases, headteachers may consider the RBA inaccessible to a pupil. In this case, disapplication may be considered. Disapplication is permitted for individual pupils who are unable to participate, even when using suitable access arrangements. Headteachers must make the final decision about whether it is appropriate for a pupil to take the RBA, and this decision should be discussed with the pupil's parents and teachers.

---

[72]https://www.gov.uk/government/publications/regulatory-framework-for-national-assessments

Pupil Mobility

18. All pupil's RBA scores will be associated with their Unique Pupil Number (UPN) and stored in the National Pupil Database (NPD). The score will therefore remain with a pupil, even if they move schools. Because scores are not shared with schools, there is no requirement to include any RBA result on a pupil's common transfer file (CTF).

Maladministration and Monitoring

19. Maladministration is monitored via the RBA digital system, and the Secretary of State reserves the right to amend or annul results should a school or individual be found to be administering the assessment incorrectly. Further guidance regarding the process for assessing maladministration of the RBA can be found in the RBA assessment and reporting arrangements, published annually.

20. To ensure that the assessment is being delivered consistently, there will be routine quality monitoring of the RBA.

RESPONSIBILITIES

Headteachers' responsibilities

21. Headteachers must sign a Headteacher Declaration Form (HDF). This must be completed once each academic year, as is currently the case for all National Curriculum assessments in key stages 1 and 2. All requirements of the HDF must be adhered to.

22. Headteachers must ensure that the RBA is being delivered in accordance with this document and the assessment and reporting arrangements which are published annually. Investigations of maladministration may result from not following the statutory guidance for the RBA.

Local authority responsibilities

23. There are no routine Local Authority (LA) monitoring arrangements for this assessment.

24. LA monitoring may be implemented as the outcome of an investigation of maladministration if a provider is found to have deliberately impacted assessment results.

Ofqual responsibilities

25. Ofqual continue to monitor the development and maintenance of the RBA as they do with all other National Curriculum assessments.

Ofsted responsibilities

26. Ofsted do not have routine access to the numerical data produced by the assessment, but individual circumstances will be considered to grant access if required for a specific purpose. The RBA should not form a part of any Ofsted inspection.

27. Ofsted will have access to individual schools' progress scores, when the progress measure is released at the end of Key Stage 2.

INTERACTION WITH OTHER ASSESSMENTS

Early Years Foundation Stage Profile

28. The EYFSP and RBA are enforced by the same legislation, however they are distinct and serve different purposes. There will be no interaction between the two assessments in practice. Schools must continue to carry out both statutory assessments.

Statutory Trialling

29. For the purpose of developing assessments in reception, a sample of schools are asked to take part in statutory trialling of the RBA. Selected schools are contacted in advance and must administer the assessment according to the trialling instructions provided.
30. Pupils who are disapplied from the RBA should not take part in statutory trials.

FURTHER INFORMATION

Useful resources

- Reception baseline assessment framework[73]

---

[73]https://www.gov.uk/government/publications/reception-baseline-assessment-framework

INDEX